PAINTED THOUGHTS

William Zackary

PublishAmerica
Baltimore

© 2011 by William Zackary.
All rights reserved. No part of this book may be reproduced, stored in a retrieval system or transmitted in any form or by any means without the prior written permission of the publishers, except by a reviewer who may quote brief passages in a review to be printed in a newspaper, magazine or journal.

First printing

PublishAmerica has allowed this work to remain exactly as the author intended, verbatim, without editorial input.

Softcover 9781456035778
PUBLISHED BY PUBLISHAMERICA, LLLP
www.publishamerica.com
Baltimore

Printed in the United States of America

To my family and friends; without all the love, encouragement and belief in me none of this would have been possible.

Contents

Painted Thoughts 7
Colours 8
Crashing Waves 9
The Dragon and the Tin Men 10
Bleached Walls 11
Silent Moon 12
Pine Island Park 13
Snakes and Arrows 14
Barricades 15
Pest 16
The Fisherman's Wife 17
Mill Yard 18
Scars 19
You and Me 20
Beautiful Bride 21
The Abandoned Coaster 22
Bless Each Day 23
Keeper of the Stars 24
Beautiful Without Trying 25
Broken Wing 26
Anger 27
Anna's Place 28
Rip Tides 29
Migrating Birds 30
Gone 31
The Last Dragon 32
Wreck of the Isadore 33
Faces 34
Something Less than a Hero 35
Into 36

She Is	37
Old 66	38
Fifty-Nine Cadillac	39
Grass Stains	40
The Grapes of Wrath	41
Amoskeag	42
In the Distance	43
Fires by the Sea	44
Woodwinds in the Grass	45
September	46
Leaves	47
Abandoned	48
I Wonder	49
Field of Rust	50
Here in the Dark	51
The Barn	52
Dead in the Road	53
The Last Wildflower	54
Tattoo	55
The Thread I Wear	56
Life is a Love Song	57
5 A.M.	58
Broken Bird	59
The Clustered Hood	60
Black and White	61
Crush Leaf	62
Tired Old Iron	63
Paper Horse	64
Fatality	65
All I Want is to Grow Old	66
Something About	67
Girls	68

Painted Thoughts

I like supersonic carbon fiber wings
My appetites titanic for life and all it brings
You like Catalina cloud-white sails full of wind
The scent of obsession, moonbeams without end

I love Euphoria, the early morning before the dew burns off
The dancing notes of a bird song, both electric and bitter soft
You love Yankee candles, aromatic rings of smoke
The moods of a rainbow wet with promise and hope

I crave autumn leaves full of color and occupied by blissful rage
The blush of a new born season as the last succumbs to age
You crave static energy, the burning deep within life's subtle glow
Calm pools of peace and harmony we both have come to know

I dream of pastel shades and smudges of charcoal across my wall
Lucent watercolors or pencil sketches, I love them all
You dream of shell cloaked beach sand and fresh squeezed lemonade
The flavors of salt water taffy and watching how it's made

We favor each other, for better or for worse
Our time is like precious metal and we crave every penny's worth
We are like the Oceans, in constant ebb and flow
We push and pull and tug at each other with our hearts in constant tow

Colours

Orange and Brown

Will come around

Along with Green and Gray

To watch Pink and Tan

Cover the land

That Purple gave away

Silver and Gold

Look rather old

In the shadow of

Yellow and Blue

While Black and White

Learn not to fight

But to love instead

No more wars

No more hate

No more

Crimson Red

Crashing Waves

Running blind into crashing waves
Patron and lime with the tides of May
Sand in my hair
Don't care about the sun in my eyes
Love last forever
In the dog days of summer
Just beyond the seas lazy ebb and flow
Lies a field of dandelions
Huddled in clusters of yellow
In this meadow of snakes and bending grass
We pass the time
With tender kisses and playful laughs
Running blind into crashing waves
Taking risk even though we are afraid
Our first kiss left me weak in the knees
Like an amusement ride often does
Or a warm summer breeze
Sleeping late into the afternoon
Fresh cut lilacs and love in bloom
Sun kissed skin both naked and insecure
Leaves me wanting less but longing for more
Time for reflection
A sense of direction
Running blind into crashing waves
Along the boardwalk or playing the arcades
Sand in my hair
Don't care about the sun in my eyes
Love last forever
In these dog days of summertime

The Dragon and the Tin Men

In the distance

Lurks the dragon

Ivory horns and jagged wings

A-fire breathing

Razor toothed battalion

Of death

And dying things

Approaching are the tin men

With their axe

And war flags drawn

But in the end

Was the wind

That was lying

Now all the tin men

Are gone

Bleached Walls

Bleached walls and pale eyes blue

Orange crush sunset view

A strapless dress

Painted in pastel shades

On something so beautiful

Only the hands of God could create

A fleeting smile

In the days aging glow

Candles burn

Summer lilies by the bed

Tequila Rose goes down slow

My eyes survey the amber curls

And soft cheekbones

Blushing red

We kiss a slow dance of affection

Retracing the thoughts

Running wild in our head

Silent Moon

The emptiness

Of a silent moon

Grips his heart

With great despair

The quite loneliness

Of a naked room

Cries of when

She was there

Hanging onto every word

That falls

From the broken stories

Of these four walls

As if all hope

Had vanished

Into thin air

Pine Island Park

They erected a fence to keep us out
It didn't work
The weeds and vegetation
Welcomed the company
I hid beneath the tree line
When cars would pass
I didn't care to be seen
Some might call it trespassing
The old coaster was rotted to the rails
Rust replaced bolts and nails
Blighted remains and charred latex
Swayed every time the wind would gust
We moved on
Through the woods to where a paved oval awaited
The cars were not there
The track was cracked and dated
I ran in circles pretending to be a race car driver
I could have used a radio flyer
We pressed on
To where a dilapidated bridge crossed a tepid canal
But all we found on the island was an empty foundation
Everything had burned to the ground years before
The day we came to explore
The pond was quiet
The airplane ride and caterpillar removed
No more giant moxie bottle to greet the guest
Now it was a part of a summer house in the neighborhood
Even the white swan boats were gone
No carousel with hand carved horses traveling around in circles
No Ferris wheel with names of famous cities
Even the drive-in theater was run down
The big screen looked like it had a frown
No pins fell in the bowling alley
The skating rink was a bloom of poison ivy
Pine needles adorned the shore where great bathhouses once stood
Time can be real harsh on fortunes and wood

Snakes and Arrows

Snakes and Arrows in my blood

No rhyme or reason why we love

Take my name and break my heart

Watch me stumble and fall apart

Tell me all about your love and pride

Anchor the knife and open me wide

Lay me down and let me go

Don't come around don't want to know

Snakes and Arrows in my thoughts

Love me now or love me not

Turn away so quick to leave

I hope you are happy

With what you did to me

Barricades

As I walk these empty streets alone

Where concrete barricades and boarded windows bloom

I am saddened to see this, my home

Once proud land of the red, white and blue

Where virgin soil has been stripped away

To asphalt and walls of multi-colored tattoos

The trees cling to life in various stages of decay

Trapped in their concrete jungle tombs

Where vacant buildings line the landscape

In the shadow of conglomerate America

Neighborhoods are besieged by murder and rape

Then left to slowly wither away

This is not the liberty I adore

This is not what so many have died for

Pest

A fleeting smile

Through tangled hair

The scent of saltwater taffy

And ocean spray

Ragged blue jeans lay

Where red roses fall

Your silk smooth skin

Beneath a parasol

A lurid sun

Blazes light years overhead

And in the presence

Of your ineffable beauty

I find myself to be

A social pariah

The Fisherman's Wife

The lines 'round her eyes are like

Ink wells full of unfinished thoughts

She pauses with brush and easel in hand

He is out to sea again with the men and tides

Working his tired fingers to the bone

Each day a little farther from shore and from home

Trying to catch the dwindling stock

The pungent smells of the sea fill the fabric of his frock

While she waits patently back on shore

With the wives of his mates

Painting lighthouses atop rocky outcrops

Trying to catch her breath

Not sleeping at night

Her eyes always looking to the sea

Anxious with the comings and goings of the waves

Longing for the texture of his touch

Missing the aroma of his company

Mill Yard

By the river she stands
Casting shadows down ancient canals
Long and narrow
Where no one ever goes
Like poison ivy shadows grow
Along thick brick red walls
And rusted wrought iron gates
In amber rays of light
The gothic mile patiently waits
The wrecking ball
Cause and effect
After years of such neglect
Alone by the river she passes
Like leaves of autumn hue
Long elegant curves
Deftly trace the land
In a hollow of guarded view
Eventually these mundane giants
Of mortar and fired clay
Will surely crumble and fall
Filling the canals
With fettering debris
While the curious come to collect
And shutterbugs call
Recording the event for history

Scars

The scars of my youth

Lay buried beneath the truth

Of what eats away at my mind

It's so clear to see

Your lack of love for me

Life sometimes can be so unkind

These walls I build around my heart

Feel cold and lonely in the dark

When all I have is questions for why

You hurt me this way

Caught in the grip of my own confusion

My heart fell for the disillusion

That you might love me one day

You and Me

Quietly beats the thunder

Of a lonely heart

Silence

The spell I am under

A world forever apart

Torn between desire and hunger

Lies the unspoken thought

Of you and me

And all we could be

And of all

We are not

Beautiful Bride

Church bells ring

We walk down the aisle

The choir sings

Everyone smiles

This is a beautiful day

You are a beautiful bride

In a small white chapel

In the lush countryside

So our journey begins

With the exchange of rings

Surrounded by family and friends

Showered with beautiful things

Our first kiss is sincere

As we are led to the door

We will celebrate this day every year

I look forward to sharing many more

The Abandoned Coaster

I remember her standing
As if it was yesterday
In a orphaned
Abandoned state of decay
Little more than crooked nails and rusted rails
Leading the way
To nowhere
She cast her twisted shadows
Along the bends in the brook
Faded and neglected narrows
Hardly worth a second of time
Never mind a second look
Waiting patiently for arson flame
Or wrecker hook
It was clear to see
She was going nowhere
So I cut through the fence and ran
For the seclusion of the pines
Their untended limbs warp
Over her elegant lines
When I reached her
Like children often do
I began to climb
To nowhere
Soon it became clear
She was too old
And far too frail
To carry the burden of my frame
Her crippled back sagged and swayed
As her legs did the same
Time and the ever changing seasons
Surely were to blame
She would carry me
Nowhere

Bless Each Day

Bless every second
We are here with you
Bless every minute
We hold onto

Bless every hour
Our good lord grants us
Bless every day
Blooms a flower so precious

Anchor the knife
Open up the world
Precious little life
Beautiful little girl

Bless each week
You change my life forever
Bless each month
For which you make me better

Bless each season
We may watch you grow
Bless each year
You're the gold at the end of our rainbow

Bless our family
For dreams which come true
Bless the stars and heavens
For the miracle of you

Anchor the knife
Open up the world
Precious little life
Beautiful little girl

Keeper of the Stars

I sat on a grassy knoll
In November of sixty-three
Felt the world burn
From Enola Gay the day she made history
I witnessed the destruction
Born in the trenches of war
I watched a giant Zeppelin
Crash and burn near the Jersey shore
I stood above a sunken Arizona
Lost forever on the seventh morning of December
I missed a berg from high in the crows nest
On a frigid night everyone can remember
I was in the shadows of the twin towers
In the haunting hours before they fell from the sky
I drove a broken down Chevy to the levy
And wept the day the music died
I've listened to preachers preach
And cynics spread the doom
I have cradled little babies
And cried alongside homeless ladies
In the abandoned streets of New Orleans
After the great monsoon
I walked beside Martin Luther
When he dared to share his dream
And soared with the crews of Apollo
Ever higher through the jet stream
I sang to the lyrics of the Beatles
When they told us to let it bleed
And sat with our elected leaders
In the house of wealth and greed
I am both creation and oblivion
Keeper of the stars
Life and death
It is what I am
It is who we are

Beautiful Without Trying

Eyes like a holiday

Mistletoe and cinnamon

Lips like chardonnay

I long for the chance to taste them

Golden locks glow with sundown

Scents of lavender and lady slippers

Wild horses at the edge of town

Picnics in evergreen pastures

Making love beneath the glow of the moon

Pounding hearts and shooting stars

Rain cools the temper of June

Alone in the shell of my car

Daffodils and dandelions

Caress your skin so fair

Beautiful without trying

Just thankful

I was there

Broken Wing

Love the bird which does not sing

Comfort the heart which knows not love

Mend thy wound, this broken wing

On bended knee I offer thee a dove

Some men come from nothing

Some men cast no stones

Some men make great dreamers

I dream of the things no man shall own

Love these days which cast no shadows

Longing for her with all your strength

Live beyond the realm and limitations of tomorrow

She only loves you at arms length

Some men wear thick skin

Some men never learn

Some men break before they bend

I smolder and burn

Anger

Anger consumes a heart grown cold

Childhood memories are lost

On a mind grown old

Black rimmed eyes and silver hair

The endless void of a barren stare

Sometimes I wonder how your blood

Could ever run through my veins

Compassion spills forth from a teary eye

Anger retreats into selfish pride

Old stories untold fade into lore

Until the blood in my veins

Boils no more

Anna's Place

The passing sun cast shadows and chrome

On window panes and weathered stone

I think of all that might have been

Look at us now and look at us then

Your house sits empty on a sleepy street

Holding tightly to the secrets it keeps

The door swings open in the stiff rolling wind

You don't love me as a son or friend

Rain begins to fall and washes down the grit and grime

But no amount of rain can wash away this pain of mine

I enter slowly with caution as I close the door

This is not your house anymore

I search through everything hoping to find a clue

Something that might link me to you

But all I find are empty shelves and four bare walls

There is nothing here to comfort me at all

Rip Tides

August haze
Hot humid days
Out to the lighthouse and back
Watching the breakers wreak havoc
Sipping a Cadillac
Wild lupine explodes
Purple patches on sides of the road
As a heavy tide rolls
Waves press hard against a craggy shore
Until the beach is no more
Rip tides carry away driftwood and debris
Without conscience
Without mercy
Back out to sea
As the Moon and Jupiter
Waltz as one across the sky
Our love is
Without question or quandary
Still our moods change our minds
Like the tides change the Oceans boundaries
Waiting for the next big wave to take us under
Always testing our faith in each other
August haze
Blissful days
Over the dunes and down to the shore
Life shouldn't hurt like this anymore
A slow kiss and then a good bye
Though the words are never spoken
What is left if everything is broken?
Into the waves
Without a second thought
Pleasure never felt this guilty
Passion never burned this hot

Migrating Birds

She likes to watch the birds migrate
Early spring to autumn late
I enjoy our walks
Into the depths of the urban woods
The sounds our footsteps make
Against the forest floor
Watching the creatures
Gathering their goods
Along a twisting path
Down to the lake shore

Where
Driftwood protrudes from ash and sand
Water laps in waves against the fertile land
Tired birds stop for a brief reprise
Resting their weary wings
Until sunrise

When
Once again they will slice
Through a milky morning sky
Beyond our reach
Or range of reason
Looking for a place to nest down
And try to carry on
For another season

Gone

Gone are the trees

With their colorful shade

Gone are the rivers

And all the life they gave

Gone are the mountains

With their peaks of rock and ice

Gone are the prairies

Wither all the wheat and rice

Gone are the storm clouds

And all the rage they hold

Gone is the sunlight

Our fire hath grown cold

The Last Dragon

Snarling, the dragon stands at the edge of his lair
Snorting volcanic fireballs high into the air
The rotten stench of war wafts from the diseased forest below
Certainly by now all the Kings armies are on the go
A winged terror to all mankind, the very last in a long bloodline
He has grown more restless with advanced age
Compassion now gives way to wounded rage
The angry serpent turns back to his cave and sifts through old souvenirs
Things he has collected throughout all his years
A discarded sword or a broken and bloodied shield
Trophies and trinkets gathered from the hell grounds of the battlefield
Alone in the dark he lights a fire with a spark of his acid born breath
Not in anger nor in blight
His yellow eyes are frosted and welcome the needed light
His search is one of panic until he finds the item he has been looking for
A torn and tattered yarn of cloth scattered about on the floor
While outside comes the metallic rumble of a blitzing war machine
So the fearless dragon rushes to the entrance to survey the carnival scene
Dawn breaks as the first sentry reaches the crest of the hill
Only to be greeted by the demonic dragon's harsh words of will
"I stand before you a mighty dragon with ivory horns to crown my head
I'm a fire breathing menace who fills your rivers with the blood of your dead
I love to creep into your dreams and rape your best kept secrets
Leaving fear and despair for you to drown in my wake
I find the human heart is the easiest of all to break"
Then he let out a terrible roar usually reserved for the hollows of war
But this dragon is worn out and wishes to fight no more
So he quietly slips back into his fortress with one last labored exhale
For he knows the Kings army will soon be hot on his trail
But there will be no epic battle on this blissful day
This dragon is deceptive and simply fades away
All the King's men will find after their flight upon the hill
Is a dragon cloaked in the Kings own white flag
His fire has cooled, his body lay rigid and heart beat forever still

Wreck of the Isadore

There is legend of a ghostly ship
In the waters near Cape Neddick light
Broken along the rocks off bald head cliff
Last of November night
She sails the icy Atlantic with a ghastly phantom crew
Like she has since her maiden voyage
In eighteen forty two
The Isidore was a barque bound for Orleans
Before she was to sail for the coast of France
But her crew was spooked
And believed it was with the Devil
She would share her final dance
One deckhand abandoned ship
While another foretold of a dream he had
Seven coffins on a pier
Six for his mates and one for the downtrodden lad
But his tale fell upon deaf ear
Soon the ship left port for the open sea
Shortly before a Nor'easter hit
And spent the night tossed about by crushing waves
Until early next morning
Where upon the rocks she split
Shortly after wreckage and bodies began to wash ashore
Seven lost souls is all they recovered
Not a single more
Among those recovered was the body of the sailor
The one who had tried to warn the others of impending doom
Before the Isadore was cast to sea
His nightmare had been a prophecy
Remember this the next time
You survey the Ocean from the leisure of shore
The ship you see in the distance
Immerging from a fogbank
Just may well be
The legendary Isadore

Faces

One face is warm and loving

The other is dark and cold

One face is young and playful

The other is worn and old

One face is commanding

One face is demanding

One face is not enough to live by

One face is brave and handsome

The other is selfish and poor

One face is polite and well groomed

The other so unkempt and unsure

One face is respectful

One face is regretful

One face is not enough to live by

No matter how I try

Something Less than a Hero

What have I learned

In all the years I have burned?

Filled with regret and remorse

At my poor choice of course

No longer the man

I was born to be

Something less than a hero

Now resides within me

Shackled to the chains

Of indecision and self doubt

I leave the rest

For you to figure out

Into

Into the water I dove
Sinking like a stone
Far below the waves and crush of life
Slicing through the surf like a butchers knife

Into the hills I drove
My worries and thoughts left at home
Down a deserted stretch of two lane road
Into the unknown I did go

Away from the light and all I know
Away from life I suppose

Into the morning I awoke
Rising to the occasion like rings of smoke
Casting my shadow proudly as if I were truly someone
Loving you with a confident aplomb

Into the day I arose
Dressed in fancy new shoes and clothes
A king to rule a new found kingdom
A prisoner granted his unconditional freedom

Away from the night and all the shadows
Into a new life I did grow

She Is

She is cold autumn rain
Tequila on an orphaned day
Grass bowing to the wind
Summer nights with a hint of cinnamon
She is opaque morning light
Dawn and dew pressed against window pane
The lyric of autumn at first light
Solitude found down a quiet wooded lane
She is a smile from a veil
A turbulent April shower
The breeze expanding a sail
A beautiful English flower
She is the ebb and flow of a restless sea by moonlight
Musical notes of brass married to strings and trumpets
The raging colors of a novelty mood ring
A free spirit is the most amazing thing
She is a tender love song
Delicate and naïve
Cloud formations of crouching lion and graceful swan
Someone who fulfills my every need
She is matinees with buttered popcorn
Sand dollars and carnal knowledge
Hardscrabble miles of cracking neon and pulsing fluorescent
Her lips press to mine with a bit of an edge
She is ash and embers dancing in the fury of the inferno
A kaleidoscope of ever changing leaves
Covered bridges discovered in mountain valleys
Always and forever
She is my love eternal

Old 66

I want to drive down old sixty-six
In a black GTO
Counting dilapidated drive-in theater screens
Wasting away along the side of the road
Following the meandering curves and vacant billboards
Of this iconic lost highway
Watching America ramble by
Somewhere between sixty and seventy
Searching to find something to call my own
Reflecting on life and how fast the kids have grown
Driving west as the sun goes down
Always awaking in a different
Little known town
I won't stop unit I reach the Pacific
Aglow in the splendor of the majestic Golden Gate
Not until I have touched the graffiti scarred walls of Alcatraz
And danced alongside the ghost of Joplin and Garcia
Around Ashbury and Haight
I want to ride old steel wheels
Through the black hills of South Dakota
Hunt caribou and fish for walleye
In the backwoods of Minnesota
Roam the halls and lawns of Monticello
Ride the Coney Island Cyclone white knuckled
I want to sprawl in the outfield grass of Wrigley field
Scale the mighty walls of Hoover dam
Hike end to end over the Appalachian Trail
Find out exactly who I am
These are the things I want to do
As long as I grace the Lords green earth
Life is too short for grieving
As long as I am on the right side of the dirt

Fifty-Nine Cadillac

I want to cruise
The crowded boulevard

Past white picket fences
Standing guard to perfect yards

With the windows down
So we can smell the salt and sea

With the stereo turned up
Listening to the thoughts of Dylan
Lennon and Springsteen

As we travel up the coast
With just our cloths in the back

Maybe spend a night or two
On a beach with a perfect Ocean view

And listen to the waves
Lap against the sand
Working on a perfect tan

Just you and me
In a cherry black

Fifty-nine Cadillac

Grass Stains

She runs wild
With the wind at her back
Her long hair trailing
Well behind in the breeze
And with the oncoming clouds
Comes the rain
To chase her further on
Down the chain
To where the prairie grass
Grabs a hold and stains
The bends in her knees
If I were a four leaf clover
Trampled on or bent over
To reveal my leafy underside
Would I catch the corner of your eye?
Or the bottom of your heal
Would I wilt and die?
All parched and bone dry
Do you have any idea how that would feel?
Or would you take me home?
In little bits and pieces
Stuck into the fabric of your cloth
All warm and soft
Until the next laundry day
When I would be washed away
Back into the river
Soon to be delivered
Back into the field
Waiting for you to run by again

The Grapes of Wrath

The grapes of wrath
Grow so fast

Along the squalid walls
Of my empty garden

The sun and rain
Nurture these needs

Quenching my thirst
With lust and greed

Until the bitter soil
Embraces the seed

With great sorrow
The thorns on the vine

Penetrate my skin
I bleed white lies

From deep within
Spilling forth

A killing contamination
Until nothing will ever

Grow here again

Amoskeag

On the shores of the river Merrimack

Below the Amoskeag falls

Elm trees sprout from granite beds

In the shadow of old brick walls

Where the Pennacook once settled

And the pale man later came

The willows by the silver river

Would never again look the same

From mortar, steel and stone

Arose the cathedrals of industry

Along the shores on either side

As far as the eye can see

Here I witness the budding leaves of spring

Among the relics of the past

Where the smile of the spirit

Today goes by steadfast

In the Distance

In the distance I see a light
A beacon in the night
Guiding me home like a savior

But the closer I get to shore
Only makes me want it that much more
Which in turn fuels the fire of my odd behavior

I have come such a long way
And I know the shore can't be far away
I can hear the breakers through the inclement weather

At times I have to wonder though
If I had tried a little harder in the beginning you know
Maybe in the long run I would have fared better

In the distance ring the notes of a horn
Hammered brass all battered and worn
A sentry in the dark just out of reach

A guide to lead me safely into shore
A reward for all the struggles I endure
I think I can see the outline of the beach

So I paddle hard with all my might
For sure enough the dunes are coming into sight
And it appears I have made it home

I have lived another day to tell my tale
About a shipwreck at sea during a winter gale
My only regret is that I came ashore alone

Fires by the Sea

The savage aroma of red wine and smoldering ash

Is an intoxicating smell against the eerie twilight glow

The yellow flame licking obsessively into the stone berth

In defiance of its man-made confinement

Haunting shadows caress the cavities of our sallow skin

The liquor begins to warm my body from within

I close my eyes and listen ever so carefully

To the soothing melody of the captured inferno

Overhead a starlit night embraces the archaic heavens

As we rest upon the salt-bleached stones

At the oceans edge

I hold you close to shield the chill of night

The sea swells in her cradle

And crashes angrily upon the muted shore

Then retreats to the safety of its cold deep hamlet

Only to chase us into the arms of each other once more

Woodwinds in the Grass

I hear the night wind blow
It doesn't sound like anything
I ever heard before
The leaves are like fine trumpets
Huddled in the trees
The crickets like wood winds in the grass
Beneath the canopy
Shards of Moon light
Break through the blinds
Melting into the infinite cracks in the floor
Cooling the room
From the drought of summer
Waking me from a deep slumber
Where it is hard to remember
The shifting sands beneath my pillars
Filled with the scent
Of nightshade and single malt brandy
Midway and lemonade
I hear the night wind creep
Ever so slow
From high on the hill
Through the thick meadow
The rhythm of water against rock
The chorus of firefly and bull frog
Erase reality
The cancer eating away within me
In those quiet times
Before the break of dawn
I am whole again
Lupine in morning rain

September

Do you recall those days of fall?

Blue skies and burning rain

Green fields we knew by name

Somehow nothing is the same

Today

One simple kiss

Soft and innocent

Though to me it meant so much more

For one fleeting moment

I had found everything in life

I was ever looking for

Leaves

Yellow, Red and Orange leaves

Fall to the ground

Where children at play

Gather 'round

Stuffing old cloths

With the bounty found

The sweet song of laughter

Is a magical sound

It rings through the trees

And passes through my window pane

Echoes off the wall

From the lawns down the lane

Creeps into our subconscious

And keeps us on a level plane

Helping us to remember

When we were kids again

Abandoned

Abandoned and neglected

Casting shadows beneath a blue sky

Crooked as a smile

By the time I gathered the courage to try

I held on tight

Fearing she might let me go

Something wasn't right

In this place

Where crabgrass and shadows grow

She felt cold

Worn down by neglect

I was too young then to know

Now I am left

To look back and reflect

They took her away a short time after

And I never touched her again

Gone were the thrills and the laughter

She was alone in the end

I Wonder

If I told you that I love you

Would you look at me and care?

If I asked you for affection

Would you know I was there?

If I kissed you softly

Would you remember my name?

If I thought about you all the time

Would you do the same?

And if I took you to be mine

Would you stay with me for the rest of our time?

Or would you pass like a summer shower?

Are you my thorn?

Or are you my flower?

I wonder

Field of Rust

Wasting away in the weeds and sand
Leeching they're way into the land
Rotting piles of multi-colored rust
Polished trophies corroding back into dust
Quietly reverting back into earth
What is death and what is birth?
Here lie the servants of mankind
In many different shapes and forms
Having reached the limits of their time
A new and different breed is born
Caught forever in snapshots of sun dried pigments
Baked to a bone pale finish
Strangling vines wrap around cracked metal grills
Like an old man's grimace
Against a back drop of engine blocks and wild blown fauna
The seeds of decay flower while the appetite of rot devour
Forever changing the landscape in this picture
Which is the poorer and which the richer?
Slowly washing away with each passing shower
The earth is cleansed and trespassed against
All in the same second, minute and hour
And each year more and more come and go
Like wild flowers in an open field
Stamped and machined legends yield
To the constant friction of the passing hour
Cast offs sent here without a second thought
Where the worn rest while the broken rot
Lending out they're parts to those who remain
Worthy of our roads and precious time
Which one is yours and which one is mine?

Here in the Dark

Here in the dark
All alone
Just flesh and blood
Wrapped around tired old bone
What do they see?
Inside of me
I wonder if they can tap
Into my memories
Here in the dark
I think of family
My flesh and blood
All the ones I love
I think of the days
When my daughters were born
So long ago
How I love them so
Here in the dark
All alone
Every fiber of my being
Begs to go home
And feel young again
Like I used to feel
When rain would fall
On my naked face
And my young legs
Were eager to race
Any and all things
Brave enough to challenge my heart
These are the things
I think of
Here in the dark

The Barn

I follow the path as it snakes through the woods
Chipmunks run across the trail well ahead of me
Somewhere far off a chainsaw rips through felled timber
Fuel for the fire of another winter

Off to my right a pond comes into view
The many colors of autumn explode along the jagged shoreline
Their outline reflects off the surface of the pool
Shades of red and yellow melt into blue

From here the sounds of the highway are not so clear
They have to duel with the songs of the forest for the interest of my ear
A sharp bend leads me to a dilapidated barn covered with brush
With a stone foundation cracked and limp

Shingles hang about and some litter the forest floor
Limbs poke through holes in the roof like fragile arms embracing the sky
I take out my paper and pencil and begin to draw
Soon scribbled lines and shadows fill the page before my eyes

Once finished I gather myself and head back on my way
Satisfied with my discovery on this afternoon
I walk briskly to the road and the warmth of my car
Anxious to see my drawing on display

Pencil and charcoal oblige and define
Paper and dust coagulate and align
Asphalt atop masonry
Nature amid decay

Dead in the Road

Cut down in the prime of life

Found you dead in the road

When the sirens came

Dropped by a bullet

In the midst of a fight

You spent your last breath

On a deserted patch of country lane

Now out in the woods

Lies a crooked white cross

It's old and decrepit

And camouflaged with ivy and moss

With a few dead and dried flowers

Scattered around a faded Polaroid

All that remains

Of a life destroyed

The Last Wildflower

Mary lies by the road

Her lipstick turning blue

When you are gone you are gone

What was I to do?

Mother hides in the garden

Planting seeds of anguish with great pain

No sun will shine this morning

Nothing can stop the rain

The last wildflower

Far too frail to bloom

Your leaves lay bare

By the time we got there

You left us far too soon

Tattoo

I wince when the needle
Digs down to the bone
The monster awakens
And bleeds some more
Large jagged wings
Dug into the small of my back
Lifeless red eyes
Threatening to attack
This is a story
Told in flesh and blood
This is a story
About trust and love
Again the needle bores down
Into the skin
Forcing more ink
Into the blend
A rattlesnake coils
Up the length of my spine
Sinking venomous fangs
I feel the swipe of a hand across my back
Blood and ink gel into a cocktail of pain
I bury my head into the fold of my arm
Convincing myself to go forward again
The sonic buzz of the gun
Hangs like smoke
Color is applied with broad swift strokes
Green for the scales
Yellow for the underbelly
The artist is perfecting an image of a menacing race
Long rows of razor sharp teeth
Splintered around a crooked forked tongue
Vibrant and agile, restless and young
Sunk into my back for the rest of my life
Another set of eyes lurks just beneath the skin
Staring back at the world with a menacing grin

The Thread I Wear

Love is the thread I wear
Not today or tomorrow but for a lifetime
I wrap it around myself like a dare
It radiates within me with a warm subtle shine
Protecting me from all I fear
Dark shadows or coming year

Love is the thread I wear
Sorrow has no path or place to penetrate
The threads are strong and sturdy here
And will not let me down
Today 'nor tomorrow shall I frown

Love is the thread I wear
Wrapped like warp from limb to limb
I gleam and gloss and run across
All that would dare to break my skin
I gather my strength from family and friends

Love is the thread I wear
In sun splashed fields were I grace
Pounding footsteps ramble forward in frantic pace
Echoes of laughter fill my thoughts
And gate my presence
Fear I not these unwanted haunts

My love is the thread I wear

Life is a Love Song

Life is a love song

A bittersweet pill we sometimes choke on

An endless letter of blissful sorrow

The blank pages of a blind tomorrow

Life is like a crushing wave

All the choices we never made

The shadows crawling

In the corner of a naked room

Church bells ringing

On a lazy Sunday afternoon

Life is like a hangover in the morning

A twisting cloud approaching without warning

Sallow skin grown over a fresh scar

Never quite sure of whom we are

A restless flight with new born wings

Life is a series of wishful things

5 A.M.

Listening to the blues
On a Sunday afternoon
With a shot of tequila and blue curacao

What was it you said?
Those words echo through my head
Seems like I spend more time in the past than in the here and now

I'm sorry if I hurt you
We used to be beautiful
Now all we do is go round and round
Abrasively wearing each other down

I speak of you in words of encomium
If there were others I guess I didn't see them
I love you more than you will ever know
This is why this hurts me so

5 A.M.
My mind is wandering again
Listening to the rain on the roof

I wonder what you're doing
What kind of life have you been pursuing?
I swear this hangover must be a hundred-proof

Broken Bird

Plastic horses sit idle
Beside decorative porcelain dolls
Ivory meadows sway in the wind
Beyond painted plaster walls
I sit alone and try to make sense of it all
Wondering where you have been
The answers don't come easily
Much to my chagrin
The tension between us has grown
As thick as thieves
What did I do to deserve that kind of reaction?
Tomorrow the sun will crest over the hill
And all these distractions
Will surely test my will
What will it matter?
If your not here with me
Just another day
To wallow in this bed of agony
If the morning never comes
Will I remain intact?
Knowing in my heart of hearts
You're never coming back
No pill or liquor bottle will ever hide
The pain now boiling up inside
It crawls up my spine
And bores into the back of my brain
Where I slowly choke on all this pain
I know you can sense the anguish
Within these words
Shattered wings can no longer support
The weight
Of this broken bird

The Clustered Hood

Everyday I come this way
Through a clustered hood with nary a wood
Asphalt and aluminum bake in the heat
Barely a soul now walks this beat
Oblivious to me climbing the single hemlock
Higher and higher to thoughts all my own
Below a lady stops to spell her weary bones
Grocery bags sagging as she descends
The bench brings comfort to her tired limbs
There is but one on this side of the lane
She waits for the trolley to arrive
In the comfort of a cigarette and chewing gum
I wish I had some
Across the lawn church bells mark the time
Reminding me I cannot stay a second longer
Soon I will be late for dinner
And being thin I have no wish to be any thinner
I can't wait to tell all about my day
Like it was some sort of great adventure
I had been contracted for
Maybe I will lie about my activities
Maybe not
I can't tell for sure
Life can be so mundane
On the other side of the door

Black and White

One is black and one is white

Is one wrong and the other right?

Why do we hate a man?

Simply for the color of his skin

And have no interest in what

He has to offer from within

I ask you this

For the hate lies in you as well as I

It's the way we were brought up to believe

Our story book heroes who hide behind paper mask

And we ourselves live behind borders

And barbed wire

And never stop to ask

Why?

Crush Leaf

There is a hole in my heart
Where I always fall in
I stumble through the day
Full of scars and short comings

You look into my eyes
Like you're peering into my soul
You hold my hand close
Like you haven't the will to ever let me go

Remember our first kiss
I was so nervous
I nearly missed

In the earliest morning light
Safe and warm in the comfort of my arms
You are everything right with my life
I was a fool to ever think
I could protect you from all harm

There is a break in the clouds
In the skies somewhere overhead
As I stare at a full moon tonight
I am haunted by all the things I never said

Looking at old photographs
Scattered about across the floor
Growing up and growing old together
Never gave much thought to the day
We would kiss no more

Remember our first kiss
I was so nervous

Tired Old Iron

Tired old iron
Rust in bloom

Bleached out whitewalls
In a cracked rearview

Shade line is crawling
Like arthritic fingers across the plain

A pale red sun beats down
On steel wheels and burned out flames

When at last before my eyes bestow
In the dying embers of a golden glow
She sleeps alone in a cradle of grass

Orphaned road king
Shadow of the past

With wings of chrome and dual tailpipes
Fender skirts and racing stripes

Stuck in the grasp of riverbed clay
Lost in a field of trophies and decay

Tired old iron
Rust in bloom

Paper Horse

Who elected me?

To be the white knight on a paper horse

A sometime Romeo

When there is no other place to go

Why is it I

Who must be your stepping stone?

Is it not enough?

That I hang like a lifeless puppet

On the end of a lovers rope

With my heart exposed

For all to see

There is no hope alive in me

Why can't you just leave me alone?

Fatality

I have seen the rain

Fall to the ground like fire

Fleeing the angry heavens above

I can feel the parched earth

Licking my dead skin in my delirium

I have witnessed the colored clouds

Circling like vultures overhead

As I drown in the quicksand

Of my Technicolor illusion

I have seen the stranger's face

And I hear the winds dying whispers

Envelope the broken vestige of my body

And I know no fear

For my Lord is here

I close my eyes and join him

All I Want is to Grow Old

All I want is to grow old

One day have grandchildren to hold

I don't need to be rich or desire fancy things

Life has more to offer than possessions can bring

All I want is to grow old

To see the day when my bones don't fancy the cold

I want to watch my children raise they're own

And be there for them should they ever need to come back home

All I want is to grow old

To be there with my wife when we reach gold

I want to walk with her on a sandy beach

With our golden years within our reach

Spoil our grandchildren like our parents did

Live my life until I have had my fill of it

All I want is to grow old

Something About

There is something about
The way you look in a simple sun dress
The scent of your perfume as it lingers
On the sheets and pillow case
The taste of your kiss as it settles on my tongue
With your hair in your eyes
How your dress comes undone
Whenever you spend the night

There is something about
The way you sound so vulnerable
While you bite my lip until I bleed
And dig your nails into my scars
The way I tremble when you turn to leave
The aroma of the morning coffee
How shallow you sometimes breathe
In the earliest morning light

There is something about
The rhapsody of when we come together
The symphony our whispers trail in the dark
Pledging our love forever
How your eyes fill with tears without warning
As our hearts ache for embrace
Catching the first ray of light dawning
Nothing ever felt so right

There is something about
The way our bodies unite as we touch
How we share the simple things
That mean so much to both of us
The dreams we share alone in the dark
As we make love
There was never any doubt
This was love at first sight

Girls

One looks like her

And the other looks like me

Two delicate flowers

In bloom on our tree

Paper dolls and teddy bears

Crayon portraits cover the walls

Ear aches and sour stomachs

The endless lines of phone calls

Madeline and the tooth fairy visit

With snow white and the spice girls

Hugs, kisses and a plethora of wishes

To my two little girls

With their hair full of curls

Would you like to see your manuscript become a book?

If you are interested in becoming a PublishAmerica author, please submit your manuscript for possible publication to us at:

acquisitions@publishamerica.com

You may also mail in your manuscript to:

**PublishAmerica
PO Box 151
Frederick, MD 21705**

www.publishamerica.com

PUBLISHAMERICA